D0722751

Chimpanzees

Written by
Helen Lepp Friesen

MEDIA ENHANCED BOOKS
AV²
BY WEIGL
ADDED VALUE • AUDIO VISUAL
www.av2books.com

MEDIA ENHANCED BOOKS
AV2
BY WEIGL™
ADDED VALUE • AUDIO VISUAL

AV² provides enriched content that supplements and complements this book. Weigl's AV² books strive to create inspired learning and engage young minds in a total learning experience.

Your AV² Media Enhanced books come alive with...

Audio
Listen to sections of the book read aloud.

Key Words
Study vocabulary, and complete a matching word activity.

Video
Watch informative video clips.

Quizzes
Test your knowledge.

Embedded Weblinks
Gain additional information for research.

Slide Show
View images and captions, and prepare a presentation.

Try This!
Complete activities and hands-on experiments.

... and much, much more!

Go to www.av2books.com, and enter this book's unique code.

BOOK CODE

F539363

AV² by Weigl brings you media enhanced books that support active learning.

Published by AV² by Weigl
350 5ᵗʰ Avenue, 59ᵗʰ Floor
New York, NY 10118
Websites: www.av2books.com   www.weigl.com

Library of Congress Cataloging-in-Publication Data

Lepp Friesen, Helen.
 Chimpanzees / Helen Lepp Friesen.
      pages cm. -- (Amazing primates)
 Includes index.
 ISBN 978-1-4896-2870-1 (hardcover : alk. paper) -- ISBN 978-1-4896-2871-8 (softcover : alk. paper) --
 ISBN 978-1-4896-2872-5 (single user ebk.) -- ISBN 978-1-4896-2873-2 (multi user ebk.)
 1. Chimpanzees--Juvenile literature. I. Title.
 QL737.C23T633 2014
 599.75'24--dc23
                                    2014039003

Printed in the United States of America in Brainerd, Minnesota
1 2 3 4 5 6 7 8 9 0 18 17 16 15 14

122014
WEP081214

Project Coordinator: Katie Gillespie
Art Director: Terry Paulhus

Contents

Meet the
Chimpanzee

Chimpanzees are **mammals**. They belong to the **order** of **primates**. Most primates have ten fingers and ten toes and can pick things up with their hands and feet. Chimpanzees are social animals. They live in groups called communities. These are made up of 15 to 120 chimpanzees.

Chimpanzees are omnivores. This means that they eat both plants and animals. They live in trees, where they find much of their food. Chimpanzees use their long arms to swing from branch to branch.

Chimpanzees walk on all four feet. This is called knuckle-walking. They can also stand up and walk upright.

All About
Chimpanzees

Chimpanzees belong to a family of animals called *hominidae*, which also includes gorillas and orangutans. There are two **species** of chimpanzee. These are the common chimpanzee and the bonobo. The bonobo is the smaller of the two.

Chimpanzees have hair instead of fur. Only the face, palms, and soles of the feet are not covered with hair. Hair helps to keep a chimpanzee warm. It also protects the chimpanzee's skin from the Sun.

Chimpanzees have big ears and can hear very well. They can also see color. Their long fingers and toes help them grasp small things.

Chimpanzees communicate with up to 30 different calls. Scientists refer to the calls of chimpanzees as pant-hoots.

Comparing Primates

Because there are so many species of primates, scientists split them into subgroups. Each of these subgroups is called a superfamily. There are six superfamilies of primates. Grouping primates makes it easier to study their similarities and differences.

Lemurs

+ **Length:**
3.5 to 28 inches
(9 to 71.1 centimeters)
excluding tail
+ **Weight:**
1.1 ounces to 21
pounds (30 grams
to 9.5 kilograms)
+ **Special Feature:**
Lemurs are the primate
at the highest risk
of **extinction**.

Tarsiers

+ **Length:**
3.6 to 6.4 inches
(9.1 to 16.2 cm)
excluding tail
+ **Weight:**
2.8 to 5.8 ounces
(79.3 to 164.4 g)
+ **Special Feature:**
Tarsiers have
the largest eyes,
compared to body
size, of all mammals.

Lorises

+ **Length:**
7.5 to 15 inches
(19 to 38 cm)
+ **Weight:**
9 ounces to 4.6 pounds
(255 g to 2 kg)
+ **Special Feature:**
Lorises are the only
poisonous primate.
They secrete a **toxic**
oil from a gland in
their elbow.

Old World Monkeys

+ **Length:**
13.4 to 37 inches
(34 to 94 cm)
excluding tail
+ **Weight:**
25 ounces to
110 pounds
(700 g to 50 kg)
+ **Special Feature:**
They have nostrils
that are narrow and
point downward.

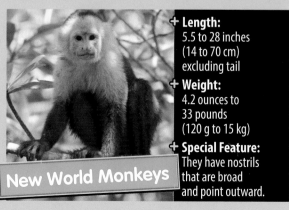

New World Monkeys

+ **Length:**
5.5 to 28 inches
(14 to 70 cm)
excluding tail
+ **Weight:**
4.2 ounces to
33 pounds
(120 g to 15 kg)
+ **Special Feature:**
They have nostrils
that are broad
and point outward.

Apes

+ **Length:**
3 to 6 feet
(90 cm to 1.8 meters)
+ **Weight:**
12 to 399 pounds
(5 to 181 kg)
+ **Special Feature:**
Apes do not have tails.
They are the most
intelligent of
all primates.

Chimpanzee History

Chimpanzees have lived in Africa for millions of years. The name *chimpanzee* was first used in the 1730s. It means "ape" in Tshiluba, an African language.

In 1960, Dr. Jane Goodall traveled to Africa to study the behavior of chimpanzees in nature. She was the first to observe that chimpanzees made and used tools. This was an important discovery, as scientists used to think that only humans used tools.

Chimpanzees use different tools for different tasks. They may use more than one tool for more difficult tasks. They also teach tool use to their infants. **Archaeologists** have found tools that chimpanzees used more than 4,000 years ago. Some of these tools are similar to the ones they still use today.

SPACE CHIMPS

In 1961, before people went into space, a chimpanzee called Ham was sent into space in a rocket.

Chimpanzees use rocks as tools to crack open nuts.

Where Chimpanzees Live

Most chimpanzees live in western and central Africa. They live in nature in 21 different countries. Chimpanzees can be found in **habitats** that range from moist **rainforests** to dry **savannas**. Chimpanzees spend much of their time in trees, where they are protected from **predators**. For sleeping, they make platform-shaped **nests** out of branches and leaves.

Chimpanzees are very sociable. They spend much of their time grooming each other. Grooming involves removing dirt, plant debris, dry skin, or insects from their own or each other's hair. Not only does grooming keep chimpanzees clean, it also serves to maintain community ties.

The size of a chimpanzee community depends on the habitat and how much food there is in the area. During the day, chimpanzees play and look for food. When the food runs out in one area, the community moves on.

There are about 100,000 to 200,000 chimpanzees living in Africa.

PREDATORS

Leopards and pythons are the main predators of the chimpanzee.

Chimpanzee Features

Chimpanzees are highly intelligent. Using tools is just one sign of this. They are also able to solve problems and understand the use of symbols. Some chimpanzees raised by humans have learned **sign language** and how to use computers. Chimpanzees are one of the few animals that can recognize themselves in the mirror.

Getting Closer

➊ Senses

- Both eyes can focus on the same object, creating depth perception
- Better sense of sight than smell

➋ Teeth

- 32 teeth
- Long canine teeth for tearing meat

➌ Face

- Short beard
- Brow ridge above the eyes
- Large nostrils and ears

➍ Hands and Feet

- Thumb and forefinger are fully **opposable**
- Can pick up objects with both hands and feet

➎ Hair

- Long, coarse, black hair
- When nervous, hair stands on end

What Do Chimpanzees Eat?

Chimpanzees eat hundreds of different foods. They eat the fruits, seeds, and flowers of plants, as well as insects, eggs, and meat. They will hunt in a group for larger **prey**, such as birds, monkeys, and small antelope.

Chimpanzees use different tools to collect food. Sticks are used to dig grubs out of a log or honey out of a hive. Chimpanzees "fish" for ants or termites with long sticks. They poke the sticks into an anthill or termite mound. Then, they lick off the insects that crawl onto the stick.

PLANT POWER

Some chimpanzees know which plants to eat when they have aches or pains, such as stomachaches.

Chimpanzees use leaves as sponges or spoons to drink water.

Chimpanzee Life Cycle

Male and female chimpanzees live together in one community. The bonds between community members can last for many years. Experts have not observed any long-term bonds between male and female chimpanzees when it comes to mating. Chimpanzees may mate at any time during the year. About eight months after mating, females give birth to either one infant or twins.

Birth to 2 Months

A newborn weighs about 4 pounds (1.8 kg). After birth, it clings to its mother's stomach for 30 days. The mother takes care of all the infant's needs. These include food, warmth, and protection.

Female chimpanzees usually have their first infant when they are 15 to 16 years old. A female will not have another child until her first infant is **weaned**. Females give birth about every five years. They usually have four to six offspring in their lifetime.

5 Years to Adulthood

From the ages of five to nine, chimpanzees slowly become more independent. They start to play more on their own. They also interact more with other community members. However, they still maintain a close bond with their mother. Chimpanzees reach adulthood at about age 15.

2 Months to 5 Years

Baby chimpanzees depend fully on their mother for the first five years. At around five or six months, infants start to ride on their mother's back. By age two, they can sit alone and travel on their own. Chimpanzees are weaned at about five years.

Conservation of Chimpanzees

The number of chimpanzees living in nature has been greatly reduced in recent decades. This is mainly due to habitat loss caused by humans. Experts now believe that chimpanzees could soon become extinct, unless they are protected. That is why chimpanzees are now listed as **endangered**.

Logging and mining both cause **deforestation.** When an area of forest is logged or mined, chimpanzees lose their homes and food supply. Their community may be forced to split up. Logging and mining may also pollute local water supplies. Hunting and the exotic pet trade are problems, as well. Since the 1990s, diseases such as **Ebola**, have killed thousands of chimpanzees, too.

CHIMP ORPHANS

Special centers take care of orphaned chimpanzees and give them a safe place to live.

Dr. Jane Goodall has worked for more than 50 years to protect chimpanzees. Much of her work has been done in Gombe Stream National Park.

Myths and Legends

Myths and legends are stories passed down over time. One such story is about large "Bili Apes" from Congo, Africa. The local legend caught the interest of scientists when a Belgian officer brought home a gorilla skull in the early 1900s. The skull was from the area of Bili in Congo. It sparked interest in the possibility of a new species of gorilla.

War in Congo prevented scientists from traveling there to investigate for many years. Finally, in 2004, a research group went to the Bili Forest to explore. They did not find a new species of gorilla. However, they did find a large community of chimpanzees that were quite different from other known chimpanzees. They are much bigger and behave more like gorillas than most chimpanzees. For instance, some of these chimpanzees nest on the ground, instead of in trees.

According to legend, Bili Apes hunted lions, caught fish, and walked upright like humans.

Chimpanzee Life Cycle

Research in the library and online to find out more about the chimpanzee's life cycle. Make notes about each of the three stages. Do you notice any similarities to other animals you know?

Materials needed: a big piece of paper, some colored markers, access to the internet

STEP 1 Draw three big circles and label them with the headings: Birth to 2 Months, 2 Months to 5 Years, 5 Years to Adulthood.

STEP 2 Draw arrows to show the correct sequence of the life cycle, as in the diagram below.

STEP 3 List the facts you have discovered inside the circle for each stage of the life cycle.

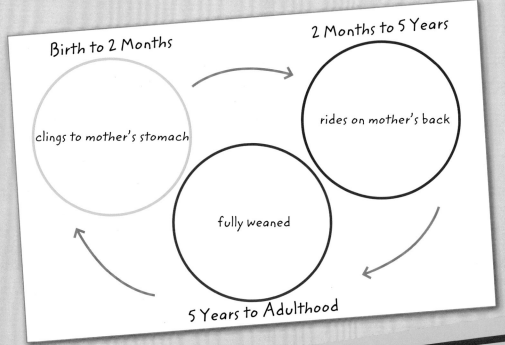

Birth to 2 Months
clings to mother's stomach

2 Months to 5 Years
rides on mother's back

fully weaned

5 Years to Adulthood

Know Your FACTS

Test your knowledge of chimpanzees.

1 How many chimpanzees usually live in one community?

2 What is the name that scientists have given to the call of the chimpanzee?

3 What important discovery did Dr. Jane Goodall make about chimpanzees?

4 About how old are chimpanzees when they reach adulthood?

5 What are the main threats to the chimpanzee population?

ANSWERS

1. 15 to 120
2. Pant-hoots
3. Chimpanzees make and use tools
4. 15 years
5. Logging, mining, hunting, and diseases

Key Words

archaeologists: scientists who study objects from the past

deforestation: clearing large areas of forest

Ebola: a deadly disease

endangered: at serious risk of no longer living any place on Earth

extinction: no longer living any place on Earth

habitats: environments in which an animal lives

mammals: warm-blooded, live-born animals that drink milk from their mother

nests: structures that animals make out of branches and twigs for sleeping

opposable: able to touch the other fingers of the same hand or other toes of the same foot

order: in biology, a level of classification

poisonous: able to produce a harmful substance to protect itself from prey

predators: animals that hunt other animals

prey: an animal that is hunted

primates: mammals with relatively large brains, flexible hands and feet, and good eyesight

rainforests: dense forests with heavy rainfall

savannas: grassy plains with few trees

sign language: a communication system that uses visual gestures, such as manual, facial, and other body movements

species: animals that share many features and can produce offspring together

toxic: harmful substance produced by an animal or plant

weaned: to have moved from drinking milk to eating food

Index

Log on to www.av2books.com

AV² by Weigl brings you media enhanced books that support active learning. Go to www.av2books.com, and enter the special code found on page 2 of this book. You will gain access to enriched and enhanced content that supplements and complements this book. Content includes video, audio, weblinks, quizzes, a slide show, and activities.

AV² Online Navigation

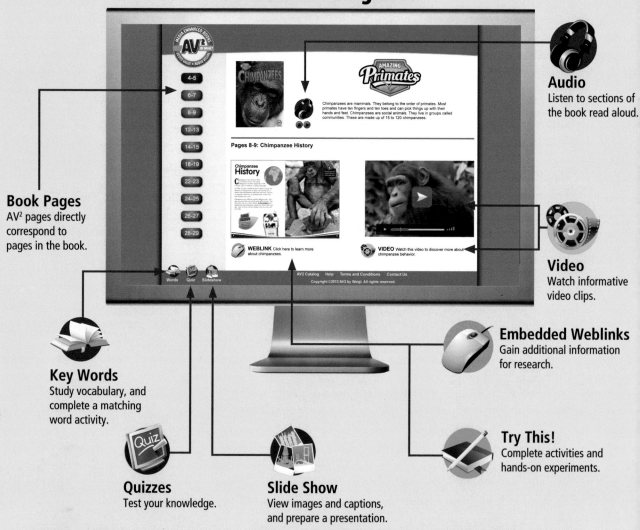

Book Pages
AV² pages directly correspond to pages in the book.

Key Words
Study vocabulary, and complete a matching word activity.

Quizzes
Test your knowledge.

Slide Show
View images and captions, and prepare a presentation.

Audio
Listen to sections of the book read aloud.

Video
Watch informative video clips.

Embedded Weblinks
Gain additional information for research.

Try This!
Complete activities and hands-on experiments.

AV² was built to bridge the gap between print and digital. We encourage you to tell us what you like and what you want to see in the future.

Sign up to be an AV² Ambassador at www.av2books.com/ambassador.